THE UNSUNG HERO
The Role and Struggles of a Stepfather

Copyright © 2025

All rights are reserved, and no part of this publication may be reproduced, distributed, or transmitted in any manner, whether through photocopying, recording, or any other electronic or mechanical methods, without the explicit prior written permission of the publisher. This restriction applies to any form or means of reproduction or distribution.

Exceptions to this rule include brief quotations that may be incorporated into critical reviews, as well as certain other noncommercial uses that are allowed by copyright law. Any such usage must adhere to the specified conditions and permissions outlined by the copyright holder.

CONTENTS

Glossary 4

Chapter 1.
What It Means to Step In 5

Chapter 2.
The Challenges of Being a Stepfather 7

Chapter 3.
The Thankless Job.. 10

Chapter 4.
When Love Feels One-Sided, and Why You Still Stay 13

Chapter 5.
Legal Recognition and Court Cases............................ 18

Chapter 6.
The Psychological Perspective..................................... 21

Chapter 7.
Strategies for Success 24

Chapter 8.
Your Legacy Is Love... 26

Chapter 9.
Overcoming Challenges and Building a Lasting Bond 29

Chapter 10.
The Power of Persistence 32

Chapter 11.
The Journey's End, A Stepfather's Reward 35

Chapter 12.
Embracing the Role, A Stepfather's Triumph 38

Chapter 13.
Moving Forward Together... 40

Chapter 14.
Nurturing the Family You've Built.................................43

Chapter 15.
Overcoming Setbacks and Finding Peace 46

Chapter 16.
The Unseen Legacy, What You Leave Behind...................... 48

GLOSSARY

- Blended Family: A family where one or both partners have children from prior relationships.
- Custody: Legal right to care for and make decisions about a child.
- Stepfather: A man married to or in partnership with a child's biological mother but not the biological father.
- Legal Guardian: Legal authority to care for another person, usually a child.
- Parental Rights: Legal rights and responsibilities of a parent regarding a child.
- Visitation Rights: Rights granted to a non-custodial parent to visit their child.
- Non-Biological Parent: An adult in a parental role who is not genetically related.
- Psychological Impact: The effect of step-fatherhood on mental and emotional health.
- Troxel v. Granville: Landmark U.S. Supreme Court case on visitation rights of non-biological parents.

CHAPTER 1
WHAT IT MEANS TO STEP IN

No one is born a stepfather.

There's no baby shower or grand welcome when you step into a child's life as a second man. You arrive halfway through a story shaped by someone else's absence, neglect, or broken promises, yet you're somehow expected to hold it all together, without a blueprint or instruction manual.

Becoming a stepfather means choosing to love without conditions.

It says, "I'm here," even when nobody asks you to be. You're up early, packing lunches; you attend school meetings where other parents look at you with hesitant curiosity. Sometimes you're the quiet supporter in the crowd at a school play, cheering for a child who may or may not acknowledge you.

You walk into a home where nothing was built with you in mind. There are photo frames that don't include your face, traditions you had no part in creating, and a child who still hopes their "real dad" will call. On birthdays, you may be just a face in the background; your presence might feel merely tolerated at holidays. But still, you stay.

And that is what sets you apart.

In time, these small acts become a legacy. One day, maybe not soon, the child you came for will look back and understand: You didn't have to be there. But you were. That made all the difference.

This role comes with a unique weight. It's not quite grief, but a quiet sense of displacement. You're asked to provide, protect, guide, and discipline, often without the acknowledgment or respect shown to a biological parent.

Navigating Pre-Existing Family Dynamics

Society has its own stereotypes about stepfathers. Too often, you're labeled the "backup" parent, the one who fills in when the biological father isn't around. But this doesn't reflect reality. Many stepfathers today are the primary caregivers, the role models and protectors, making contributions equal to, or even surpassing, those of a biological father.

CHAPTER 2
THE CHALLENGES OF BEING A STEPFATHER

There's a special weight that comes with being a stepfather, a burden few will see, but one you always carry. It's not just about being present; it's about being enough.

Enough to fill a gap you didn't create.
Enough to love and protect, but without full authority.
Enough to keep giving, even when the child still longs for someone else.

It's not a mourning of what's lost, but a longing for what's rarely named. You offer your strength like roots beneath the soil—anchoring, invisible, essential. You guide and guard, often without reward, your role etched not in title, but in the small, unnoticed moments where love is shown, not spoken.

Navigating Pre-Existing Family Dynamics

One of the first challenges is resistance. Stepchildren may push back for many reasons, loyalty to their biological father, fear of change, or confusion about where they fit in the new family structure. You enter a dynamic that never included your face in old photos, often with a child who still hopes their "real dad" might return. Your presence is a reminder that something fundamental has shifted, and not every child is ready to accept that.

Building trust with your stepchildren is an agonizingly slow process. Many stepfathers face the pain of being seen as "second-best" or just a substitute. But trust is never built through grand gestures; it's earned through patience, consistency, and compassion, day after day.

Building Trust and Respect

People think they know your story. They assume you're just the man who stepped in when someone else walked out. But what they don't see are the sleepless nights, the patient conversations, the football games and scraped knees, the tears you catch and the joy you nurture. You're not a placeholder—you are the place they run to. And the love you give? It's not secondhand. It's foundational.

Respect isn't demanded, it's earned through showing up, even when you don't feel appreciated. It comes from being the constant in a time of instability. Over time, the child begins to see that you're not here to replace anyone but to offer stability, love, and guidance.

Managing Relationships with the Biological Father

Co-parenting adds another layer. If the biological father is still involved, emotions can run high. Stepdads often walk a tightrope, balancing boundaries and authority. Sometimes, the biological father sweeps in with gifts or attention, leaving you sidelined. Yet, when the excitement fades, it's you who remains for the hard days and the quiet nights.

Clear boundaries, both legal and emotional, are essential. Honest communication and mutual respect for each parent's role can help foster a healthier environment for everyone. These boundaries protect your heart and sanity, allowing you to weather the moments when you feel like an outsider in your own home.

The Emotional Toll on Stepfathers

The most hidden cost is the emotional exhaustion. You work to make relationships thrive, sacrificing daily in ways that go unseen. It's easy to feel invisible, giving everything, yet getting little in return.

The outside world, your partner, even your friends, may not see your struggle. Society expects you to be strong, stoic, and unwavering, holding everybody together. Sometimes that strength comes at the price of your own well-being.

The burden can feel crushing when you're struggling to connect with a child who resists you, or you're simply trying to be heard. You keep showing up, with no accolades and little thanks. Sometimes, you find yourself asking: Is it worth it?

But here's the truth: carrying this weight doesn't make you weak. It means you're entrusted with something sacred—the future of a child's trust in love, in men, in family. Even when your sacrifices seem invisible now, one day they will be recognized.

The Weight of Step-fatherhood: A Sacred Burden

You may feel isolated and unappreciated. You may wonder if any of your effort matters. But you carry this weight because you know it's necessary. You didn't step in for praise or recognition. You stepped up because someone needed to. Because you were called.

That is the legacy of a stepfather.

CHAPTER 3
THE THANKLESS JOB

Let's be honest, being a stepfather might be the most thankless job a man can take on.

There's no manual. No training. No celebration when you step into these shoes. You're expected to do everything a father does, without the built-in respect or acknowledgment. You nurture, guide, provide, and sacrifice, but often, there's no credit when things go right.

The job is clear: be there, fill in the gaps, and anchor the family. Here's the tricky part: all of these efforts are often met with silence. There are no parades, no cards. Rarely do you hear "Happy Father's Day" or "Thank you for everything you do."

Instead, there's a quiet, never-ending hum of expectation: "What have you done for me lately?"

Sometimes your partner doesn't see your struggle. Sometimes the child resents your very presence, wishing you weren't there instead of their biological dad. Sometimes, even friends and family ask why you give so much to "someone else's kid."

Feeling alone, overworked, emotionally drained, and misunderstood is all too easy. You give and give and wonder if it's making any difference.

Here's the thing: you don't need a trophy. You're not looking for applause. You just want to know your sacrifices matter. You need to feel that the child sees you, the time, effort, and love you pour into their life.

Sometimes, it stings when you realize you won't get the recognition.

You buy new shoes for them, but they thank their mom.
You attend conferences, and the teacher assumes you're an uncle.
You stay up late planning for their future, then wake up feeling invisible in their present.

Yet, despite the lack of recognition, you stay.

Because this job isn't about applause, it's about impact.

You stay because you understand this is a long game. The child may not thank you today, but years from now, they will remember. They'll remember the small things, the quiet consistency, and the everyday acts of love.

They'll remember who helped with their homework when it got hard.
Who taught them to ride a bike?
Who was there when their biological dad wasn't?

Most of all, they'll remember you stayed, even when it felt like they didn't care.

That's the gift hidden in this thankless job: it builds a legacy.

You may not have your name on a birth certificate, but your impact is woven into their story. Your presence, sacrifices, and love shape the person they become. Even if that child never says thank you, the difference you made will last.

You may never be celebrated. But someday, when the child is wiser, they'll look back and realize what you did for them.

They may never speak your name in gratitude,
Not in the rush of youth, not when praise comes easy.
But one day—when time softens pride and ripens memory—
They will look back.

They'll see not the absence of noise,
But the presence of your silence.
Not just a man who entered their world,
But the one who never left it.

You were the shadow that stood steady,
The quiet constant in the storm.
Not seeking applause—just offering love,
Again and again.

CHAPTER 4
WHEN LOVE FEELS ONE-SIDED, AND WHY YOU STILL STAY

There will be days when you feel like you're pouring love into a well that never echoes back.

You extend love with open hands and receive shrugs in return. You speak gently, offering guidance carved from patience, only to be met with silence or sideways glares. Your sacrifices stack quietly—time you can't reclaim, money you didn't plan to give, energy pulled from your reserves—and yet what greets you is not thanks, but indifference. Sometimes, it's even rejection. And still, you stay. Not because it's easy, not because it's rewarded, but because somewhere beneath the resistance, you believe your love is building something lasting—even if no one says so.

But you are not failing.

You're investing in someone else's healing. And healing is never instant.

They're still grieving the parent who left, or worse, idolizing the one who didn't stay. They're building walls where you're trying to plant roots.

And yet, you stay. Because you know that love isn't about what comes back; it's about what you give. Even when no one sees it, even when your effort is invisible. You stay because a real man doesn't walk away from a child who needs him, even if that child doesn't realize it yet.

The Invisible Tug-of-War

Stepchildren often yearn for their absent biological parent, even when that parent is inconsistent, disengaged, or even harmful. This longing isn't betrayal, it's grief. Their biological parents shape a child's first sense of identity, and when one of them disappears or fails them, a child may internalize the absence as, *I must not be enough*.

In their heart, they continue to chase that absent parent's love, sometimes for years, sometimes for a lifetime. They're seeking validation, approval, and the affirmation that they are worthy of love. This longing can make it hard for them to accept the love you offer. They're not rejecting you, they're struggling to heal from a wound you didn't cause.

How It Hurts the Stepfather

Meanwhile, you sacrifice everything.

Your weekends.
Your sleep.
Your finances.
Your heart.
Your time with your own children.

And still, you're treated like a stranger, or worse, a villain.

"You're not my real dad."

Five words that cut deeper than silence, reminding you that no matter how much you give, you may never fill the void left by an absent father.

It's frustrating. But you stay because you know the love you give isn't just for today, it's for their future. You're investing in their healing. They may not appreciate it now, but it will shape who they become.

Personal Sacrifices and Their Impact

Research confirms that stepfathers often face emotional burnout from unreciprocated investment.

Psychology Today **notes** that children in blended families sometimes idolize absent parents as a shield against abandonment.

According to the University of Virginia's Center for Children and Families, children often redirect their anger or pain toward the available caregiver because it's safer than confronting the pain caused by the parent who left.

The American Academy of Pediatrics states that stepfathers who invest heavily and receive little affection in return are particularly vulnerable to emotional burnout, especially when they have biological children who also feel neglected.

These sacrifices can leave you feeling emotionally drained, isolated, and unappreciated. But you are not failing. You're planting seeds that, one day, will grow into understanding and appreciation.

The Guilt and Jealousy of Your Own Children

There's another layer of complexity: the feelings of guilt and jealousy from your own children. Your kids might feel left behind, less important, or sidelined. They see you attending your stepchildren's games and functions while missing theirs. You might spend more money and attention on your stepchild, creating an unintentional imbalance.

These shifts can hurt your own children, causing emotional distance and straining your bond with them. The dynamics are complicated and rarely discussed, but acknowledging this imbalance is necessary. It doesn't mean you love your biological children any less; it means you're balancing the needs of two families while trying to build trust with your stepchildren.

Why Children Yearn for Their Absent Parent

Children long for:

Origin: The parent who gave them life.

Identity: The person they want to see reflected in themselves.

Approval: The parent's acceptance and validation.

Even an underwhelming or absent parent can hold immense emotional power. A child doesn't understand inconsistency or neglect, only the deep-seated hope: *Maybe they'll show up this time.*

That longing is not about logic; it's about the heart, a heart that yearns for something that may never come.

And Where Does That Leave the Stepfather?

You feel expendable, a man doing everything for a child who may never acknowledge it. The exhaustion of giving more than you receive can make you question your worth:

"Why am I trying so hard?"
"Why do I feel guilty when I discipline them?"
"Why am I more involved than the man they call 'dad'?"

You may pull away, not just from your stepchildren, but even from your biological children, out of guilt, confusion, or fear.

So, What Should You Do?

Acknowledge the Ache: Name your pain and seek support from your partner, friends, or a counselor.

Balance Better: Make intentional time for your biological children.

Give Without Attachment to Outcome: Love without expecting anything in return. You're planting seeds, not expecting applause.

Be Consistent: While your stepchildren pursue the ghost of their absent parent, remain grounded in love and consistency.

The Long-Term Payoff

The child may never say thank you today. But in 10, 20, or 30 years, your presence will echo in their character, choices, and relationships.

You will be the foundation that helps shape them. Even if they never say the words, your love will live on through them.

And when they become parents themselves, they will understand. They'll look back and see who you truly were, not just the man who showed up, but the man who stayed.

CHAPTER 5
LEGAL RECOGNITION AND COURT CASES

The Legal Rights of Stepfathers

Stepfathers face a unique, challenging legal landscape. While society increasingly values the role of stepfathers, the law doesn't always keep up. Stepfathers do not automatically have legal rights over their stepchildren, which can create major challenges, especially in matters of custody, visitation, and guardianship.

Unlike biological parents, stepfathers often have to navigate complex processes, such as adoption or legal guardianship, to formalize their relationship with a child. These processes are rarely simple and often require the consent of a biological parent or a court's determination of what's best for the child.

Notable Court Cases and Legal Precedents

The following key court cases have begun to reshape the legal recognition of stepfathers:

Troxel v. Granville (2000):
While this Supreme Court case focused on grandparents' visitation rights, it opened the door for broader consideration of non-biological caregivers, including stepfathers, in custody and visitation disputes.

DeShaney v. Winnebago County (1989):
This case clarified that non-biological parents who act as primary caregivers could be held responsible for a child's well-being, establishing important legal ground for stepfathers.

In Re Marriage of Krempin (1999):
This case highlighted the role of a stepfather in the upbringing and custody of a child. It helped establish precedent for recognizing stepfathers' involvement in custody arrangements, especially where the biological father was absent or less involved.

Ellis v. Ellis (2002):
Here, a court awarded custody to a stepfather over the biological father, finding that the stepfather had developed a deeper, more meaningful relationship with the children and had shown greater commitment to their welfare.

How These Cases Have Shaped the Legal Landscape

These and other cases have slowly moved the law toward greater recognition for stepfathers. While stepfathers still lack automatic legal standing, courts are increasingly willing to acknowledge the emotional and physical investment stepfathers make in their stepchildren's lives.

Progress is slow, and the need for clearer protections remains. Laws must adapt to evolving family structures so that stepfathers can navigate legal challenges with the same rights and protections as biological parents.

The Role of Stepfathers in Family Law

Stepfathers are vital members of countless families today, especially in blended or remarried households. Courts increasingly recognize the emotional bond between a child and a stepfather, particularly if the biological father is absent.

Future changes in legislation may further protect stepfathers, acknowledge their pivotal role and helping ensure they are not overlooked or marginalized. As blended families become more common, it's likely that the law will continue to evolve, providing more clarity and consistency for stepfathers who are deeply involved in raising children.

CHAPTER 6
THE PSYCHOLOGICAL PERSPECTIVE

The Psychological Impact of Step-fatherhood

He did not arrive with fanfare. There was no guidebook for this kind of love—the kind that grows in silence, that is tested before it's trusted.

He walked into a life already in motion, into rooms where his name wasn't etched in memory, where every smile had a history, he hadn't lived. And yet—he stayed.

In the quiet moments, he wondered if he was enough. Not born of blood, yet pouring out heart and breath and effort to build something that didn't come with blueprints.

He gave without being asked. He protected without being praised. And some days, when his voice wasn't heard, when the door didn't open for him first, he felt the ache of being unseen.

But still—he stayed. Because real fathers are not always titled by biology. They are defined by devotion,
carved into the story by the consistency of their care.

The Importance of Counseling and Support for Stepfathers

Given these emotional and psychological challenges, counseling and support are vital. Stepfathers often feel a profound isolation, believing they can't speak openly about their struggles. Society tends to view their role as secondary, which only increases a sense of loneliness. For stepfathers to thrive, it's crucial to have a space where they can share their feelings and experiences.

Support groups, online forums, and counseling services give stepfathers the chance to talk candidly about their journeys. Counseling can help them address struggles with identity and guilt and gain a better sense of their importance in the family, even if that role goes unacknowledged. These resources equip stepfathers with tools for coping and building healthier relationships with their partners and stepchildren.

The Psychological Benefits for Children with Involved Stepfathers

Despite the hurdles, the presence of an involved stepfather offers deep psychological benefits for children. Kids with caring stepfathers tend to develop greater emotional security and self-esteem. The stepfather's consistent care helps fill emotional gaps left by an absent parent.

These children are more likely to form healthy relationships as adults. They learn the value of stability, seeing what it means to have someone show up reliably, not just when it's easy, but especially when it's hard. This consistency becomes the bedrock of their own emotional well-being.

Case Studies and Professional Insights

Psychologists and family therapists have witnessed firsthand the impact a committed stepfather can have on children and the family. In families where stepfathers are present and engaged, children tend to thrive emotionally and psychologically, especially compared to children lacking a stable male role model.

Therapists observe that stepfathers who establish a supportive and patient presence in their stepchildren's lives often face less resistance over time. This is most effective when the stepfather avoids rushing the relationship and simply provides steady, caring support. Therapy often helps stepfathers understand family dynamics and offers them practical tools to manage expectations and frustrations.

Success stories are plentiful in families where stepfathers persevere, ultimately forging deep and lasting bonds with their stepchildren. These relationships endure, showing what unconditional care can look like, even when it's not immediately reciprocated.

CHAPTER 7
STRATEGIES FOR SUCCESS

Building Trust with Stepchildren

Trust is the cornerstone of step-fatherhood, and it takes time to build. As a stepfather, you may feel like you're working behind the scenes, constantly proving your worth and hoping for your stepchildren's affection. The path to trust is slow, often fraught with setbacks, but consistency is what makes the difference.

Stepchildren might not always know why you're in their lives or why they should trust you. The wounds of losing or missing a biological parent often run deep, making resistance common. Respecting boundaries is crucial: honor their space and their emotional process as they work through their own feelings about the family. With patience and persistence, you'll lay the groundwork for trust.

The key is simple: show up repeatedly, even when your efforts seem to go unnoticed. Over time, your daily actions and quiet sacrifices will shape their views. They'll see that you're here not out of obligation, but by choice. And slowly, that trust will take root and grow.

Effective Communication with Your Partner

Open communication with your partner is essential for long-term success as a stepfather. You and your partner are a team, and maintaining that partnership is critical, especially as you navigate the complexities of blended family life.

Make it a priority to discuss your challenges, frustrations, and emotions. Regular conversations about parenting roles and expectations help prevent misunderstandings and foster a sense of security for everyone involved. Be honest about your needs and let your partner know where you require more support. A partnership built on honesty and open communication enables both of you to handle challenges with greater understanding and respect.

CHAPTER 8
YOUR LEGACY IS LOVE

Legacy Beyond the Moment

Legacy isn't measured by material possessions or the contents of your will. The truest legacy is found in the hearts of those you touch. As a stepfather, your impact may not be celebrated with fanfare or recorded in family lore. But it lives on in the unseen ways, how your children treat others when nobody's watching, how they understand love, and, someday, how they parent their own children. Those are the marks you leave behind.

You teach by example, whether it's recognized or not. Your legacy shines through your calm during storms, resilience in the face of teenage anger, and willingness to forgive even when hurt. It's present in every meal you cook, every bill you pay, every piece of advice you quietly offer. Above all, it's in your unwavering choice to stay, even when leaving would have been easier.

Your legacy echoes.

When the child you raised becomes an adult, they'll remember the man who showed up, not just for his own children, but for them. Perhaps they'll say, "He wasn't my father by blood, but he was more of a dad than anyone else."

Don't measure yourself by gratitude received today. Measure by seeds planted, storms endured, and the man you choose to be, day after day, without applause. Your legacy isn't perfection. It's love. And that is enough.

When the Line Is Crossed: A Quiet Goodbye

Sometimes, even the strongest stepfathers reach a breaking point, not from weakness, but from being human. Sacrifices build up. Patience is stretched thin. There are moments when love is met not just with indifference, but with pain, sometimes, even violence.

When a child lashes out physically, when your love is returned with anger instead of forgiveness, you're forced to face a hard truth: you can love a child deeply and still need to step away.

This isn't abandonment. It isn't retaliation. It's survival. There comes a point when loving them costs more than you can endure, and that is never a price you should have to pay in silence.

Few talk about the stepfather who stares at the steering wheel, fighting tears after being attacked by the child for whom he's sacrificed so much. Few see how he questions his very worth, wondering how the protector became the target.

Even then, he doesn't stop caring. But he recognizes that love can't heal what the other person refuses to acknowledge. So, he lets go, not of love, but of the struggle. He steps back, not out of indifference, but out of self-preservation. Sometimes, real love means knowing when to walk away with dignity.

Even as he leaves, he leaves a legacy: restraint, grace, and the wisdom that sometimes, loving someone means letting go.

Karma, Wisdom, and the Echo of Love

Life has a way of teaching lessons in unexpected ways. One day, the child who resented your efforts may become a parent or step-parent themselves. In that moment, they'll experience rejection or indifference from a child they adore. And in that humility, they may finally realize:

"This must be how he felt..."

That's not karma for revenge. It's karma as wisdom, a fuller empathy, a deeper understanding. Maybe your name will echo in the lessons they share with their own children, not as the man who gave up, but as the man who gave everything he had, and left before he lost himself.

If this is your story, know this:

You are not a failure.
You are not forgotten.
You are not unloving.

You are a man who gave what most never could. You stepped away, not because you stopped caring, but because you finally chose to care for yourself.

"Even love has limits when it comes at the cost of one's own peace. Sometimes, the bravest act of love is letting go.", Anonymous

CHAPTER 9
OVERCOMING CHALLENGES AND BUILDING A LASTING BOND

Embracing the Complexity of Step-Parenting

Being a stepfather is never simple. The path is often littered with doubts, setbacks, and, at times, outright rejection. But these challenges don't define you; they're simply part of the complicated journey of stepping into a child's world.

Step-parenting can feel like an uphill battle, with friction and one-sided effort. Children may still yearn for their biological parent, making relationships feel especially tough when their love seems to go unnoticed or unreturned.

Patience will always set you apart. Not just patience for your stepchildren, but for yourself. Day by day, your love and consistency will forge a bond that outlasts the toughest seasons.

The Power of Patience and Consistency

Building a deep bond with your stepchildren takes time, and consistency is essential. Children, especially those navigating the aftermath of a broken home, need proof that they can trust you. They're not simply adjusting to a new family dynamic, but to a new emotional reality.

For a stepfather, this means showing up regardless of how rocky the relationship feels. Whether you're at a parent-teacher conference, cheering from the stands, or offering a listening ear, each act counts. Your steady presence builds security, teaching the child you're someone who stays.

Setting Boundaries for Healthy Relationships

A lasting bond relies on healthy boundaries. You must respect both your stepchildren's emotional space and your own needs. Set boundaries early, with your partner and with your stepchildren to maintain a supportive, balanced environment for all.

It's about being present, without overwhelming the child or losing yourself. When boundaries are respected, relationships grow stronger, free from pressure or resentment.

Communicating with Your Partner: The Foundation of Success

Communication with your partner is the bedrock of step-parenting success. You are a team. Without mutual understanding and support, the challenges only multiply.

Openly share struggles, frustrations, and moments of victory. Honest discussions about parenting roles, expectations, and emotional needs ensure you both remain unified. When you and your partner move in tandem, the difficult moments become easier to navigate.

When the Going Gets Tough: Resilience in the Face of Adversity

Step-parenting can be deeply exhausting. Sometimes you'll question if it's worth it, especially when the payoff isn't visible. It's normal to feel discouraged, but perseverance matters more than perfection.

Progress may feel slow, but the resilience you build through adversity is what forges lasting, meaningful relationships. The bond won't form overnight, but every loving step echoes far into the future.

The Ripple Effect: Your Efforts Are Never Wasted

Every effort you make to be there, love, and support ripples outward. Your stepchildren will one day carry your lessons forward. They'll look back and see the importance of someone showing up, consistently, lovingly, and unconditionally.

In time, your relationship will evolve from one of duty to one of genuine affection and lasting respect. Even in hard moments, the love you gave will shape how they view themselves, their future, and all their relationships.

Planting Love, Reaping Years

When things are tough, keep the long term in mind. Your investment isn't just for today; it's building their future. The emotional stability and care you provide will help your stepchildren grow into resilient, emotionally secure adults.

Your bond with your stepchildren may become one of the most rewarding relationships in your life. The love, lessons, and sacrifices you give will endure in their stories. One day, they'll look back and realize: you didn't just show up, you stayed.

The Gift of Consistency and Love

Never forget: your presence matters. Your love isn't a quick fix; it's the bedrock of a lifelong relationship. Step-parenting isn't easy and isn't always recognized, but its impact will last long after you're gone.

The relationship you build today sets the stage for your stepchildren's future. They'll carry your lessons forward, teaching their own children the value of stability, love, and perseverance. In their hearts, they'll remember the person who chose to stay, even when it was hard. They'll know you gave more than love; you gave a legacy.

CHAPTER 10
THE POWER OF PERSISTENCE

Endurance in the Face of Doubt

Step-fatherhood demands patience and resilience. Early days are often filled with resistance, confusion, and emotional turmoil that can be deeply discouraging. It's natural to wonder if your sacrifices and love will ever be truly seen or reciprocated. Doubt may creep in; you may question whether any of this makes a real difference.

But in the long run, persistence is your greatest ally. Being a stepfather isn't an exercise in instant gratification; it's a long-term commitment, an investment in a child's life and in your relationship together. True rewards rarely arrive overnight; they reveal themselves with time, consistency, and a refusal to let temporary setbacks define the journey.

You will face challenges that feel impossible. There will be backward steps and moments when it seems progress is slipping away. These episodes do not determine your worth. Persistence, your unwillingness to give up, ultimately shapes the bond you're building.

The Long-Term Benefits of Perseverance

The beauty of perseverance is that it doesn't depend on immediate rewards. The effort you put in today may not be seen for years, but its effects will resonate well into the future. Even if praise is slow or absent, what you do leaves a permanent mark on your stepchild's life.

Children with consistent, involved stepparents develop greater emotional stability, self-esteem, and resilience. These strengths extend into adulthood, helping them cultivate healthy relationships and strong coping skills when life gets tough.

Your steady presence, especially when uncelebrated, lays the groundwork for these outcomes. That presence becomes the security and stability your stepchildren need. One day, they will look back and realize the true significance of your daily sacrifices.

When to Ask for Help: Finding Support

Persistence doesn't mean you have to face everything alone. The bravest thing you can do is reach out when the burden feels overwhelming. Seeking support is not weakness, it's wisdom. Whether you talk to your partner, trusted friends, or connect with support groups, sharing your challenges brings perspective, relief, and often solutions.

Many resources are available: in-person and online support groups, professional counselors, and communities of stepfathers ready to listen. Building a strong network helps you stay grounded, ensuring you're not just surviving but growing through this unique journey.

Dealing With Setbacks and Moving Forward

No relationship path is perfectly smooth. There will be times when your stepchildren pull away, test boundaries, or make you feel invisible. These moments are not signs of failure; they're part of the process.

Every setback is an invitation to grow. Each time you persevere through frustration, you strengthen your emotional resilience, deepening the connection you share. Real love is rarely loud. It's the consistent, often unnoticed care that makes the greatest difference.

Celebrating the Small Wins

In step-fatherhood, it's the little victories that count most: a child calling you "Dad" after years of silence, a shared laugh, a first request for advice or comfort.

These moments may seem small, but they're monumental. They prove that your love, persistence, and presence are transforming lives. Each one builds the foundation of your lasting legacy.

Your Legacy Is Built on Persistence

Stepfathers seldom get the recognition they deserve. Society, and sometimes even family, overlook the incredible effort required. But your legacy is found not in applause, but in quiet moments: early mornings, long nights, patient persistence.

You are building something that lasts. Even if your stepchildren don't realize it yet, your steady presence is shaping their lives and the future of your family.

One day, they'll look back and realize: "You were always there, even when I didn't see it."

That is your legacy, and it's worth every ounce of perseverance.

CHAPTER 11
THE JOURNEY'S END, A STEPFATHER'S REWARD

The Long Road to Recognition

Becoming a stepfather is not a path paved with ease or certainty. There are no maps, no medals, only the quiet forging of a man beneath the weight of unseen sacrifices and unanswered questions. Each day adds another layer to your soul through missed expressions of gratitude, silent tears, and the steady heartbeat of presence. You'll walk through storms without a forecast, offer love without invitation, and still return, day after day, because love built on choice is the purest kind. Applause may never come, and the world may never pause to honor your role.

Even the children you pour yourself into may not fully see your sacrifices—at least not now. But this journey was never about the stage lights. It's about the small sacred moments: the hand they reach for in fear, the glance of trust at the dinner table, the lesson they remember in your absence. One day, when you least expect it, you'll realize this was never about raising someone else's child—it was about shaping a bond that will ripple through every choice they make. The reward? It lives in the echo of your effort, in the love that endures, and in the legacy, no one saw you build—but one they will one day carry forward.

The True Reward: Love and Legacy

Real reward comes not in public acknowledgment, but in the quiet moments, your legacy is written in love. It lives in the sacrifices no one saw: late nights, missed opportunities, steadfast strength.

Ultimately, your legacy is the gift you leave the world. It's about what's etched in memory, not what's written in a will. Your influence carries forward: in the children you've raised, the lessons you've taught, the ways you've shown up. It's about being remembered as the person who stayed when others didn't.

You have planted seeds of love that will bloom for years to come.

The Ripple Effect of Love

You may sometimes wonder if you're making a difference, especially when a child doesn't recognize your sacrifices. But every loving effort, large or small, ripples outward. Your commitment creates security, and your example teaches what true, unconditional love looks like.

One day, your stepchild will grow to value showing up, not just when it's easy, but when it matters most. When they become parents themselves, they will pass down the lessons of love and resilience you gave them.

The Ultimate Reward: A Loving Relationship

Time deepens the relationship between a stepfather and his stepchild. What starts as a fragile bond can blossom into enduring trust and genuine love. The foundation you lay today delivers a reward not measured in thanks, but in the strength of the connection you forged.

One day, perhaps as adults and parents themselves, your stepchildren will see everything differently. They'll realize you didn't just fill in; you chose to love and to stay. The lessons you taught will pass to another generation, and your legacy will echo in every act of love.

Your Reward Is the Love You Gave

Step-fatherhood may not bring instant or public reward. It is a path of quiet sacrifice and steady persistence. But the greatest gift of all is the lasting bond that stands the test of time.

It may take years for your stepchildren to understand everything you gave. But when the time comes, when they look back and see you were the one who stayed, they'll understand your love and your legacy.

You were never just the man who showed up. You were the man who built a bond, who stayed, and who gave a legacy of love that endures for generations.

CHAPTER 12
EMBRACING THE ROLE, A STEPFATHER'S TRIUMPH

A Role Like No Other
Being a stepfather is like stepping into a story already in progress. You join at a point where routines are set, bonds are formed, and previous wounds may linger. Unlike biological fathers who witness the story from page one, you arrive in the middle, with all its challenges and opportunities.

From the outside, step-fatherhood can look thankless, lacking the built-in affection or respect that often comes with being a biological parent. But when embraced fully, this role can be deeply fulfilling. It demands patience, persistence, and unwavering commitment. In return, it offers the chance to shape a child's future and to influence generations beyond your own.

The Triumph of Presence
Success as a stepfather isn't found in accolades, acknowledgment, or grand gestures; it's in the quiet, consistent presence that fills the gaps in a child's life. It's found in listening when they need to talk, showing up for their games, offering support when your partner's overwhelmed, and simply being there through the highs and lows. The most successful stepfathers know their steady presence is the backbone of a loving, resilient family.

The Emotional Transformation
The growth that comes with step-fatherhood is profound.

The journey constantly asks you to adjust, empathize, and support stepchildren who may have endured loss or hurt. You become more than a provider or protector; you become an emotional anchor.

Stepfathers live through a paradox: providing love and stability while accepting that their love might not be returned right away. Emotional resilience is essential, understanding that love, though sometimes invisible, is never wasted. The most powerful changes often happen quietly, beneath the surface, as you help shape your stepchildren's hearts.

Fulfilling the Role of Protector and Guide

You're not just a father figure; you're a mentor and a source of stability in a sometimes-chaotic world. Whether teaching life skills, giving advice, or offering a safe place to land, your influence helps stepchildren become secure, well-adjusted adults. Even in hard times, your wisdom will guide the future they create for themselves.

Building a Foundation for the Future

Every effort you make lays the groundwork for your family's future. The example you set, the support you offer, and the lessons you share will stay with your stepchildren for life. Your love and values become a blueprint for their future relationships, and one day they'll look back and recognize the gift you gave.

The Legacy You Leave

Your legacy as a stepfather won't always be recognized in the moment. You may not hear "thank you" today, but your efforts matter. The kindness you show, the sacrifices you make, and the lessons you teach will echo long into your stepchildren's lives, shaping their choices, relationships, and the way they raise their own children.

Your legacy doesn't stand in the spotlight or ring out through applause. It lives in quiet places, rooted in the hearts you've nurtured with patience and love. It's reflected in the laughter you inspired, the guidance you gave, and the strength you offered when no one else did. Not carved in stone but held in memory, your impact remains steady, soulful, and everlasting.

CHAPTER 13
MOVING FORWARD TOGETHER

The Journey Beyond the Struggles

Step-fatherhood is often painted with moments of both triumph and frustration, but its true essence lies in moving forward, as a family. The road can sometimes feel long and uncharted, filled with emotional potholes, miscommunications, and unspoken expectations. It's easy to get lost in day-to-day challenges, feeling unappreciated, exhausted, or isolated.

Yet even in the difficult moments, moving forward is the goal, to treat each day as a new opportunity to shape the family dynamic and continue growing together.

Adapting to Change

Family life is a journey in constant evolution. What worked yesterday may not work today. Children grow, their needs shift, and you may find yourself constantly adjusting to these changes. Your role will evolve as the family does, especially as your stepchildren mature and their emotional needs change. Your relationship with them will also need to adapt and grow.

One of the most vital strategies for moving forward is adapting to change. Flexibility and the willingness to meet new family challenges head-on are essential. Past struggles don't define your future. Focus on how you can contribute to positive change as your family grows.

Dynamics may sometimes feel tense or uncertain, but resilience and adaptability allow you to rebuild trust and navigate ups and downs. Be prepared to accept that your relationship with your stepchildren will look different at different stages of their lives, and that's okay. They will grow, and so will you. Your reliable presence is the constant foundation upon which everything else is built.

Maintaining Respect for the Biological Parent

One of the most challenging aspects of step-fatherhood is balancing respect for the biological parent while carving out your own place in the family. Children may struggle with loyalty to their biological parent, especially early in the blending process. They may see you as a threat or intruder, making your role all the more complex.

Maintaining respect for the biological parent is crucial. It creates stability for the children. It teaches them that respect and collaboration hold everything together, while families can look different. Co-parenting doesn't require agreement on everything, but it does require prioritizing the children's needs, especially their emotional health.

The impact can be profound when biological parents can set aside differences for their children's sake. Kids benefit from the example of healthy co-parenting and gain vital security. As a stepfather, you can support this process by fostering good communication between parents and supporting your partner in all co-parenting challenges.

Strengthening Your Relationship with Your Partner

The heart of a strong family is a strong partnership. Your relationship with your partner forms the foundation of your family's dynamic. Yet this partnership can often take a backseat to children's needs, the stresses of blended family life, and daily responsibilities.

Nurturing your partnership is as important as your connection with the children. Without it, navigating the family unit becomes even harder. Open, honest communication is the key. As a stepfather, emotional burdens may sometimes go unnoticed or misunderstood. But a united front between you and your partner offers consistency and respect to your stepchildren, showing them what a healthy partnership looks like.

Check in with each other regularly, discuss challenges, wins, and emotional needs. Share frustrations, joys, and concerns, and carve out time for connection. Prioritize one another, even on the busiest days. A strong partnership ensures your family has the support it needs to thrive, even during tough times.

The Importance of Patience and Time

The road ahead won't be perfect. Some days will bring joy and progress; others will bring roadblocks. Patience is your greatest guide. Although it may seem slow, time has a way of healing wounds, building trust, and deepening connections. With patience and consistent love, your efforts will bloom into lasting relationships.

As a stepfather, trust the process. Even when everything feels stagnant, your presence, effort, and love shape the future. The bonds you build today will last into tomorrow.

Creating a Stronger Tomorrow

Moving forward as a family doesn't mean forgetting past struggles. Instead, it's about learning from them and using that wisdom to create something stronger. The patience, love, and resilience you invest now will shape your family's future, just as past choices have molded the present.

Step-fatherhood is a continual process, a journey, not a destination. Together, your family grows, each member contributing to the overall health of the dynamic. Your commitment today builds a more unified and harmonious family tomorrow. The future is shaped by what you do now. And that future is brighter when you move forward, together.

CHAPTER 14
NURTURING THE FAMILY YOU'VE BUILT

Creating Strong Bonds From the Start

Building a family as a stepfather is unique and often challenging. Unlike biological parents who bond with their children from day one, you enter a family with established routines, relationships, and histories. Still, your role is central in nurturing those relationships and establishing a strong family foundation where every member feels valued and loved.

Success lies in fostering connection: finding common ground, creating shared experiences, and showing up, especially when it's hard. Stepchildren may not immediately embrace you; the journey to a deep bond can take time. But patience and steady effort lay the groundwork for love, unity, and emotional health.

Strategies for Nurturing Your Family

Create Traditions
Traditions are a powerful way to bond. Rituals give the family emotional landmarks, creating connection and inclusion. Traditions don't have to be grand; consistency and togetherness are what count.

Holidays offer natural opportunities for memory-making. Decorating together, sharing special meals, or watching a favorite movie establishes a sense of belonging. Weekly family activities, movie nights, brunches, or outings build a routine of connection and laughter.

Traditions become the fabric of shared experience. In blended families, these rituals forge unity and teach stepchildren that family is not just about genetics, it's about commitment and love.

Use Positive Reinforcement
Positive reinforcement is one of your most powerful tools. Take time to celebrate every family member's achievements, not just your biological children. Honor big moments and small victories. Cheering on your stepchildren, whether for good grades or small breakthroughs, builds self-esteem and shows that they matter to you.

Offer love and support in difficult moments too. Teach resilience through encouragement, even after setbacks. Even when it seems unnoticed, your support plants seeds for lasting, trusting relationships.

Strengthen Family Bond Through Conflict Resolution
Conflict is inevitable in any family, but it can be uniquely complex in blended families. As a stepfather, you set the tone for disagreement by modeling healthy, respectful conflict resolution. Lead by example, respond with patience and empathy, let everyone feel heard, and seek solutions together. Your approach will teach your stepchildren communication, empathy, and problem-solving.

The Role of Emotional Availability
Emotional availability is vital. Be present, listen, and show up in both good and bad times. Stepchildren may carry invisible emotional burdens. By offering a safe space to share their feelings, you build trust and contribute to their emotional well-being.

Celebrating the Small Wins

Don't underestimate the power of small victories, a hug after a hard day, a shared meal, or asking for your advice. These moments reflect the love and trust you're building. Celebrate them. Every effort, no matter how small, counts.

Nurturing Your Relationship With Your Partner
The health of your relationship is the family's foundation. Prioritize your partner, maintain open communication, and show appreciation. When your partnership is strong, it teaches children about healthy, loving relationships and gives them a sense of security.

CHAPTER 15
OVERCOMING SETBACKS AND FINDING PEACE

Navigating the Storms of Step-fatherhood

Every stepfather faces moments when the journey feels too hard, strained relationships, co-parenting battles, or a sense that their sacrifices go unseen. The key to successful step-fatherhood is not avoiding setbacks, but learning how to respond. Your resilience, emotional strength, and ability to find peace amid adversity define your role.

Embrace Vulnerability: A Strength, Not a Weakness

Overcoming setbacks starts with vulnerability. There's no shame in being frustrated, tired, or overwhelmed. Admitting your limits and sharing them with your partner or a trusted confidant opens the door to healing. Vulnerability is a cornerstone of healthy relationships and teaches your stepchildren that expressing emotions is a strength.

Learn from Challenges: Every Setback Holds a Lesson

Each challenge is a teacher. Disagreements, conflicts, or difficult co-parenting situations can help you understand your stepchildren's needs, reveal areas for better communication, and foster growth. Look for the lesson, not the defeat, in each hardship.

Practice Self-Care: Recharge for the Journey

To keep giving, you must care for yourself. Prioritize rest, time for hobbies, and support from friends or professionals. Set boundaries, say "no" when needed, and remember that self-care isn't selfish; it's essential for showing up with strength and stability for your family.

Building Resilience: The Strength to Keep Going

Resilience is the backbone of success. It lets you weather storms, keep loving when it's hard, and model emotional strength for your children. By bouncing back from tough times, you teach your family that real love persists.

The Ripple Effect of Overcoming Setbacks

Your perseverance sets an example. Each challenge you overcome strengthens not just your relationship with your stepchildren but the emotional foundation of your entire family. They will one day recognize and learn from your ability to stay committed, even when it wasn't easy.

The Peace That Comes From Perseverance

Finding peace isn't about avoiding conflict, but managing it gracefully and calmly. Prioritize balance, self-care, and inner peace, knowing that your impact isn't defined by perfection, but by presence and persistence.

CHAPTER 16
THE UNSEEN LEGACY, WHAT YOU LEAVE BEHIND

The Power of Quiet Impact

In the fast-paced world we live in, it's easy to get caught up in seeking recognition, the accolades, the awards, the applause. In the role of a stepfather, however, your legacy won't be measured by any of these things. Instead, **your legacy is defined by the quiet, enduring impact** you've had on your stepchildren's lives. It's not the dramatic moments or the public gestures that matter most; it's the **consistent love**, the **small sacrifices**, and the **values** you've instilled in them over time.

Your legacy is built on **what you do every day**. It's in the quiet moments when you choose to be present, even when your presence goes unnoticed. It's in the love you offer, often without any expectation of return, and in the lessons you teach that will last far beyond your time with them.

You may never hear "thank you" today, but in the long run, your stepchildren will look back and realize the **depth of your influence**. The steady, consistent love you gave them is the foundation upon which they will build their own futures.

Teach Unconditional Love

One of the most profound gifts you can give as a stepfather is the **lesson of unconditional love**. Through your actions, you teach your stepchildren that love isn't earned by perfection; it's given freely and without reservation. By choosing to love them, even when they might resist or push you away, you demonstrate what it means to love without expectation.

This lesson of **unconditional love** will stay with them throughout their lives. As they grow and enter their own relationships, they'll carry with them the lesson you taught them about **true love**, love that is patient, kind, and unwavering, even in the face of difficulty. They will know in their hearts that love isn't contingent on biology, but on the **decisions you make every day to show up, care, and stay**.

In a world that often conditions love on behavior or bloodlines, you teach them that real love is not transactional, it's a choice. The **unconditional love** you have given them will empower them to love others in the same way, creating a cycle of love and acceptance that they will carry forward to the next generation.

Shape Future Relationships

The way you treat your stepchildren today will shape their relationships tomorrow. As a stepfather, you are modeling **what healthy relationships look like**, not just as a parent, but as a partner, a friend, and a provider of emotional support.

By showing them what it means to have a healthy connection, you offer them a blueprint for how to form and nurture their own relationships in the future. Whether it's the way you **handle conflict** with their biological parent, the way you **show patience** when they struggle, or the way you **support them in their dreams**, you are teaching them how to treat others with respect, compassion, and understanding.

Your stepchildren may not immediately recognize the value of your presence. Still, they will carry the lessons you've taught them into their relationships with **partners, friends**, and eventually, **their own children**. The healthy dynamics you foster in your home will break negative cycles, offering them the opportunity to create their own positive, loving families.

By choosing to positively influence their lives, you create a ripple effect that **extends far beyond your family**, influencing how they approach relationships and parenthood in the future.

The Long-Term Impact of Consistency

While your sacrifices might feel invisible in the moment, the **impact of your consistency** is immeasurable. The long-term effects of your persistent love, patience, and commitment will resonate **long after your time together**. Your stepchildren may not always recognize or appreciate your efforts, but they will **carry the weight of your love with them**, consciously or unconsciously, for the rest of their lives.

Your love will be **woven into the fabric of their identity**. Every sacrifice you made to ensure they were safe, loved, and supported becomes part of who they are. Even when life gets difficult, they will look back on the stability you provided and remember that **love** was the constant, a love that never faltered, even when things weren't easy.

The love you give as a stepfather will become the foundation upon which they build their futures. **Your persistence in loving them, despite the challenges, will create a stable emotional foundation** that they can rely on in their own lives. This emotional resilience will influence the choices they make, the relationships they form, and the families they create.

Your Legacy Is Love

In the end, **your legacy is not defined by the number of grand gestures**, but by **the quiet, consistent moments of love** you offer over time. It is found in **every act of patience**, every moment of support, and every time you showed up, even when the road was hard. Your legacy is love: the kind that endures, the kind that is not based on external recognition or reward.

The love you give as a stepfather will live on in your stepchildren's hearts. It will guide them as they make decisions, as they raise their own families, and as they choose to love others. They will one day reflect on your relationship and realize how much you shaped who they became. Even if you don't get the praise or recognition you deserve today, your legacy will remain forever in their hearts.

The true measure of your success as a stepfather isn't about **immediate acknowledgment** or **public recognition**. It's about **the quiet power of your love**, a love that will continue to echo through generations, influencing the lives of your stepchildren, their children, and beyond.

When You've Given All You Can

And sometimes, your legacy isn't just in the moments when you stay. It's in the moments when you **choose to step back** for your own well-being. There will be moments when the love you give may not be returned, or when the strain of caregiving becomes too great. But even in those moments, you're leaving a legacy, one of **self-care**, of **knowing when to protect your peace**, and of understanding that sometimes, **letting go** is the most loving thing you can do.

As you step back, you show your children the importance of **self-respect** and **boundaries**, teaching them that love does not mean sacrificing your happiness or mental health. It's about finding the balance between **love for others** and **love for yourself**. And in doing so, you create a legacy that speaks to the power of **honoring your own worth** while still giving selflessly to others

www.ingramcontent.com/pod-product-compliance
Lightning Source LLC
Chambersburg PA
CBHW062052280426
43661CB00088B/749